OXO (17)

## DATE DUE

**Leaving My Homeland**

# A Refugee's Journey from

# South Sudan

Ellen Rodger

 Crabtree Publishing Company
www.crabtreebooks.com

# Crabtree Publishing Company
## www.crabtreebooks.com

**Author:** Ellen Rodger

**Editors:** Sarah Eason, Harriet McGregor, and Janine Deschenes

**Proofreader and indexer:** Wendy Scavuzzo

**Editorial director:** Kathy Middleton

**Design:** Jessica Moon

**Cover design and additional artwork:** Jessica Moon

**Photo research:** Rachel Blount

**Production coordinator and Prepress technician:** Ken Wright

**Print coordinator:** Margaret Amy Salter

**Consultants:** Hawa Sabriye and HaEun Kim

Produced for Crabtree Publishing Company by Calcium Creative.

Publisher's Note: The story presented in this book is a fictional account based on extensive research of real-life accounts by refugees, with the aim of reflecting the true experience of refugee children and their families.

**Photo Credits:**

t=Top, bl=Bottom Left, tr=Top Right

Shutterstock: A7880S: p. 6b; Brothers Good: p. 6c; Everett Collection: p. 29tr; Vlad Karavaev: pp. 24, 25; Lawkeeper: p. 29tl; Macrovector: p. 3; MSSA: p. 28; Paskee: p. 14; Punghi: pp. 4–5b, 4t, 7, 15, 18, 20–21c; Rvector: p. 18bl; Seita: p. 1; What's My Name: pp. 10–11b; John Wollwerth: pp. 8, 9, 10, 11, 13, 16; Ziablik: p. 8b; UNHCR: © UNHCR/David Azia: pp. 23, 26; © UNHCR/Andrew McConnell: p. 19; © UNHCR/Jiro Ose: p. 27; © UNHCR/Michele Sibiloni: p. 22; © UNHCR/Catherine Wachiaya: p. 20; Wikimedia Commons: Steve Evans: p. 12.

Cover: Shutterstock: Macrovector.

## Library and Archives Canada Cataloguing in Publication

Rodger, Ellen, author
 A refugee's journey from South Sudan / Ellen Rodger.

(Leaving my homeland)
Includes index.
Issued in print and electronic formats.
ISBN 978-0-7787-3676-9 (hardcover).--
ISBN 978-0-7787-3699-8 (softcover).--ISBN 978-1-4271-1973-5 (HTML)

 1. Refugees--South Sudan--Juvenile literature.  2. Refugees--Canada--Juvenile literature.  3. Refugee children--South Sudan--Juvenile literature.  4. Refugee children--Canada--Juvenile literature.  5. Refugees--Social conditions--Juvenile literature.  6. South Sudan--Social conditions--Juvenile literature.  I. Title.

HV640.5.S9R63 2017      j305.9'0691409629      C2017-903585-1
                                                C2017-903586-X

## Library of Congress Cataloging-in-Publication Data

CIP available at the Library of Congress

# Crabtree Publishing Company
www.crabtreebooks.com      1-800-387-7650

Printed in Canada/092017/PB20170719

**Published in Canada**
**Crabtree Publishing**
616 Welland Ave.
St. Catharines, Ontario
L2M 5V6

**Published in the United States**
**Crabtree Publishing**
PMB 59051
350 Fifth Avenue, 59th Floor
New York, New York 10118

**Published in the United Kingdom**
**Crabtree Publishing**
Maritime House
Basin Road North, Hove
BN41 1WR

**Published in Australia**
**Crabtree Publishing**
3 Charles Street
Coburg North
VIC, 3058

# What Is in This Book?

# Leaving South Sudan

South Sudan is a new country in East Africa. The people of South Sudan have lived through many **conflicts** and wars. South Sudan became **independent** from the country of Sudan in 2011 after **civil wars** in the country. More than 1.5 million people died in the wars. Four million people fled their homes. Today, South Sudan is living through a civil war that began in 2013.

## UN Rights of the Child

Every child has rights. Rights are privileges and freedoms that are protected by law. **Refugees** have the right to special protection and help. The **United Nations (UN)** Convention on the Rights of the Child is a document that lists the rights that all children should have. Think about these rights as you read this book.

Many South Sudanese children have been forced to live in refugee camps.

Juba is the capital of South Sudan. It is situated on the Nile River.

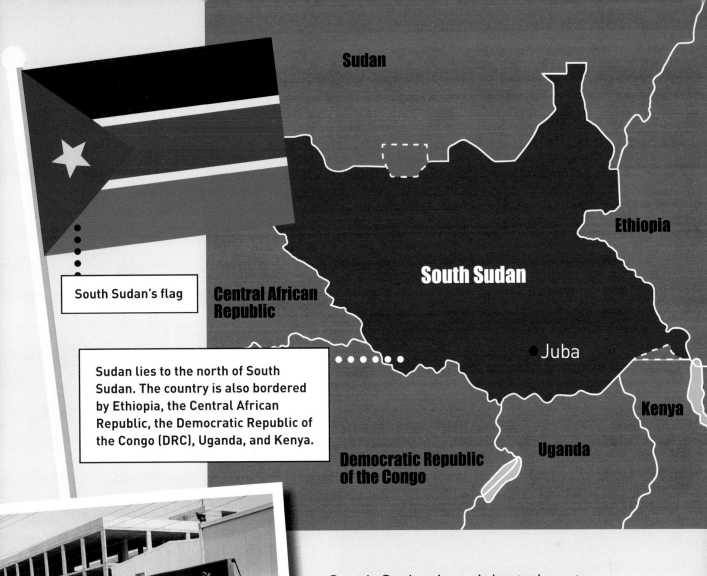

Sudan

Ethiopia

South Sudan

Central African
Republic

•Juba

South Sudan's flag

Kenya

Sudan lies to the north of South
Sudan. The country is also bordered
by Ethiopia, the Central African
Republic, the Democratic Republic of
the Congo (DRC), Uganda, and Kenya.

Democratic Republic
of the Congo

Uganda

South Sudan is a violent place to
live. People have left their homes
to save their lives. They escaped to
areas of the country that are safer.
These people are called **internally
displaced persons (IDPs)**. Many have
also traveled to neighboring countries.
They are refugees. Refugees are
people who flee their **homeland**
because of conflict. They are different
from **immigrants**. Immigrants choose
to leave to seek better opportunities
in a different country.

# My Homeland, South Sudan

South Sudan has grassy savannas, or grassy plains, and tropical forests. The White Nile River flows from the south to the north through the country. Swamps rich in wildlife line the river's banks.

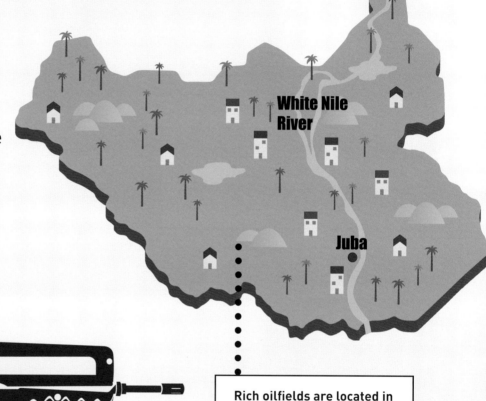

White Nile River

Juba

Rich oilfields are located in parts of South Sudan.

People coming from what is now Egypt began to settle in the area about 1,000 years ago. Other groups also arrived from nearby lands, settling as farmers and cattle herders. Today, there are more than 60 different **ethnic groups** in South Sudan. They speak many different languages and may follow traditional African religions, Christianity, and Islam. The largest ethnic group is the Dinka.

South Sudan was once part of one larger territory called Sudan. Over many years, Sudan was **invaded** and ruled by other **empires**. In 1956, Sudan became an independent country.

The Sudan People's Liberation Army is the name of the army in South Sudan.

Even before independence, Sudan's south and north were at war. The people of the north ruled the country. The south wanted more control. Southern **rebel** and **militia** groups were at war with the government. The First Sudanese Civil War (1955–1972), left half a million people dead. In 1983, the Second Sudanese Civil War began. It lasted 22 years and killed two million people. After that war, the south gained more control of its territory. In 2011, the people of the south voted to separate from Sudan. They formed a new country called South Sudan.

# Ataui's Story: My Life Before War

My people are Jieng. We are also called Dinka. In my country, we were great cattle herders. Father had many cattle. You could say he was rich in cattle. My older brother Deng helped my father with the herd.

I was born at home in my village, which is north of Adok, a city in central South Sudan. We lived near the great river, called the White Nile. I have a younger sister Grace, and a baby brother named Luol. It is my duty to look after them. We play together. In my village, I worked in our garden and fields with my mother and grandmother.

There are many fish in the great river, including Nile perch. People catch them for food.

In my land, there is a rainy season and a dry season. The rainy season is from May to November. My people plant and harvest vegetables, **millet**, and grain during that season. December to April is the dry season. Some of the men and children travel many days with the cattle to grazing camps, where the cows eat in big fields of grass. Deng looked after the cattle there, and I milked them every day.

At my village home, I liked to hoe in the fields with my grandmother. She told me stories about the lion who was a cattle stealer, and about the woman who lived with a rat. That was my favorite story. My grandmother was very wise. She told me I must learn the stories so that one day I can tell them to my grandchildren.

Students wear uniforms at some schools, but not everyone can go to school.

# Conflict in South Sudan

The years of conflict have been difficult. After South Sudan became a country, the rebel and militia groups continued to fight with the new government for power. In 2013, the president of South Sudan accused his former vice president of trying to get rid of him. He said the former vice president wanted to take over. This led to violence between supporters of the president and supporters of the former vice president. A civil war began.

The current conflict has caused around 300,000 deaths. Different ethnic groups usually support one side of the conflict. This has caused fighting between ethnic groups with different loyalties.

Both sides of the conflict rely upon the support of soldiers and rebel militia. They are all poorly paid, or not paid at all.

Government troops and militia groups also raid villages. A raid is a surprise attack. They take the children to use as child soldiers. Nearly 2.3 million people have fled their homes to avoid the violence.

With villages empty, no crops are being planted. Troops have also set fire to crops. The loss of crops has led to **famine** in parts of the country. People are starving because of the war. They are dying of diseases caused by hunger.

This tank was damaged in the fighting and has been abandoned. This is a common sight in South Sudan since the beginning of the civil war.

## South Sudan's Story in Numbers

More than

# 16,000

children as young as 8 years old are child soldiers in South Sudan. Forcing children to be soldiers is against international law.

# Ataui's Story: Village Under Attack

Men with guns came to the cattle camp to steal our cattle. Deng and the other boys were given guns to protect our herds. My father did not want me to go to the camp anymore with Deng. He said it was too dangerous. I stayed in the village.

My country has had many wars. There was fighting even when my grandmother was a girl. My grandmother said you can sometimes smell the fight in the air, like the smell of rain on the soil. One day, the rebel army came to raid my village. My grandmother said we must run to the river.

Men and boys often carry guns to protect their cattle from raids. Cattle are important to people's way of life.

## UN Rights of the Child

Children have the right to be alive and be protected.

My mother carried Luol. I grabbed Grace. People scattered everywhere. There was screaming and shooting. My mother told me to keep running, and not look back. When we stopped, we saw my father had been shot. We could not find my grandmother.

The wetlands, or swamps, along the White Nile are known as the Sud.

The bullet went through my father's back. He bled from his belly. My father told us to leave him. "You must keep going! You must help your mother keep your brother and sister safe," he told me. He knew he would soon die and the men with guns would come looking for us.

My mother was strong. She took us away. We hid in the swamps by the river. During the day, we were up to our necks in the water holding Grace and Luol. We did not know where Deng was out with the cattle. My mother cried and cried. She let her tears roll into the river.

# Fear and Survival

About 40 million people around the world are internally displaced. To be displaced means to be forced to leave your home. People who are internally displaced are living somewhere else within their home country. They walk long distances to reach safety. Sometimes, they go to nearby towns or cities. If they are lucky, they can find protection at camps run by the UN. These are internal displacement camps.

The UN helps people in need around the world. It gives emergency food, shelter, and medicine during times of war or natural disaster.

When people flee their homes, they do not take much with them. This family is living in a makeshift shelter with no safety or privacy.

This boy is selling onions in an internal displacement camp. The money he earns will help buy better food for his family.

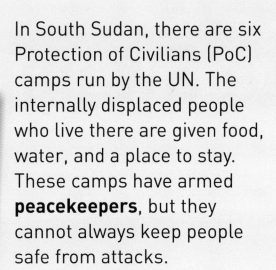

In South Sudan, there are six Protection of Civilians (PoC) camps run by the UN. The internally displaced people who live there are given food, water, and a place to stay. These camps have armed **peacekeepers**, but they cannot always keep people safe from attacks.

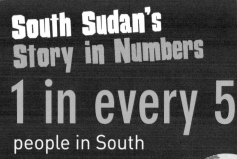

Government and opposition forces have raided the camps. They have attacked many IDPs and some aid workers there.

Some of the camps have **aid organizations** that give medical help. Doctors Without Borders/Médecins Sans Frontiers (MSF) is a group that gives medical treatment to people in South Sudan's PoCs. The group runs small hospitals when it is peaceful enough to do so.

# Ataui's Story: Leaving the Swamp

We were in the swamp for one week. Other people from my village were there, too. One night while we were sleeping, my grandmother came. We were so filled with joy. She brought my four cousins. My aunt and uncle were missing. She did not know what happened to them. All she knew was that she lost us when the village was attacked. She found my cousins hiding in the bush.

I thought of Deng. Was he still alive with the cattle? I wanted to go home, but I was scared. What if the men with guns came again?

A man fishes in the White Nile River using a pole made from a branch. The fish will help keep him from starving.

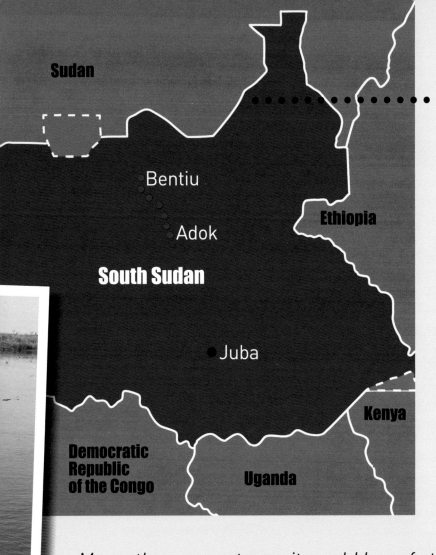

Sudan

Bentiu

Adok

South Sudan

Ethiopia

Juba

Kenya

Democratic Republic of the Congo

Uganda

Ataui and her family must walk more than 50 miles (80 km) from the swamp near Adok to Bentiu Camp.

*There was very little food in the swamp. We caught some fish by hand. We ate water lily bulbs. Two of my cousins became sick. Grace was very tired and weak. My mother and grandmother heard of a place we could get food and be safe. It was called Bentiu Camp and it was run by the UN. We would have to walk a long way to get there.*

*My mother was not sure it would be safe to try. But if we stayed, we would all die from hunger. She carried Luol. My cousin Joshua carried his sister Rebekkah. My grandmother carried my cousin Teng. I carried Grace when she was tired, and my cousin Achol walked with me.*

## UN Rights of the Child

Children have the right to care and protection if they are adopted, in foster care, or with a guardian.

# No Life for Children

The PoC camps have been open since the civil war began in 2013. They were supposed to be temporary. The UN thought that people could soon return to their villages, but the fighting continues.

The camps are very basic. Thousands of people live in tents or shabby metal shelters with tarp roofs. Open **sewers** run through the narrow alleys between shelters. In the rainy season, the camps are muddy and difficult to walk through. They are usually surrounded by a fence with barbed wire, but people can come and go as they please. If they leave, their safety is not guaranteed.

People walk for days to reach the camps. They collect drinking water in rivers and streams along the way.

**Rations** of food and water are given to people living in the camps. Meals may include a dish of sorghum (a type of grain) and split peas. People collect water from central taps or pumps. They haul the water back to their shelters in plastic jugs.

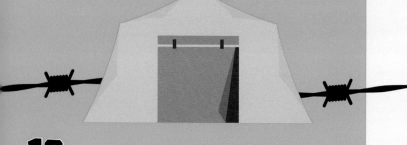

# UN Rights of the Child

Children have the right to protection from **exploitation** and **abuse**.

Many women go outside the camps to buy food and collect firewood. Some have been attacked and **assaulted** by army troops or militias. UN troops inside the camps carry guns to protect people and themselves. Even so, the violence sometimes reaches the camps. Bor Camp was attacked by government troops in 2014. Sixty people were killed. Malakal Camp was attacked in 2016, and 30 people were killed.

Some camp shelters are makeshift tents of tarps and blankets.

# Ataui's Story: Long Walk to Safety

*My feet were my soldiers. I ordered them to walk. "Feet, you must take me to the camp. I do not care if you are hurt or tired," I said. So, I walked many days. We did not have any food. We were eating leaves just to stop the hunger pains. Grace was getting weaker. Achol helped me carry her. At night, we slept under a tree or near bushes. Finally, we made it to the UN camp.*

A South Sudanese boy walks to a refugee camp in Uganda. Most refugees walk for days to find safety.

You have the right to help from the government if you are poor or in need.

Grace, Rebekkah, and Teng were taken to the camp hospital. Doctors there gave them drugs to get better. The doctors said we were all malnourished. That means we were sick from not eating good food.

The aid workers give us food and water at the camp, but it is not enough. We get millet, lentils, cooking oil, and salt. My grandmother searches for firewood outside the camp so she can cook. She sells some so she can have money to buy us more food.

IDPs carry their daily ration of water back to their shelters in a UN Protection of Civilians camp.

We have a small house at the camp in the section with other Dinka. The house has metal walls. We all sleep on the floor. It is very crowded. There are not enough toilets for everyone who is here. We must line up to use them. Sometimes, the little ones cannot wait that long to go to the bathroom.

# Some Countries Welcome Refugees

Over the years, many refugees have left South Sudan. Each time war or fighting breaks out, people are displaced from their homes. Most people travel long distances on foot. They find safety in the neighboring countries of Uganda, Sudan, Ethiopia, DRC, and Kenya. Often, they go to refugee camps in those countries.

These South Sudanese refugees helped grow this rice on a Ugandan farm.

The refugee camps in Uganda are overflowing with South Sudanese. There, they are registered as refugees and given ration cards for food and a tent to live in. To register means that the UN records who you are, where you have come from, and why. Some camps vaccinate children from diseases such as measles and **cholera**. It is easy for diseases to spread in crowded camps. In one Ugandan camp, refugees were given plots of land to plant vegetables to eat and sell.

Refugees rest in a Ugandan camp reception center after arriving from South Sudan.

Some South Sudanese refugees have reached other areas of the world. In the United States, there are 100,000 people of South Sudanese background. There are about 17,000 living in Canada. Most of these refugees arrived years ago during the civil wars when South Sudan was part of the Republic of Sudan. Today, it is very difficult for South Sudanese refugees to be accepted by any country outside of Africa. Their best hope for a better life is an end to the war.

## South Sudan's Story in Numbers

Uganda is home to

# 698,000

South Sudanese refugees.
Ethiopia is home to

# 342,000

South Sudanese refugees.

**23**

# Ataui's Story: My Home in the Camp

The camp is our home now. We have no other home. We have been here three years. My father is dead. We do not know about Deng. I think about him all the time. In my dreams, he is alive and looking after our cattle. I do not want to think that he is dead or that he has been forced to join the army as a soldier. If he is gone, our cattle will be gone, too. Our cattle were our life.

If we see someone from our village at the camp, we ask them if they have any news of home. The answer is always no, or that things are not good. Some people want to leave to go back, but it is too dangerous. Here, we just exist and hope that the fighting will stop soon. But at least we have food and we are all alive.

The conditions in the PoC camps are not good. But they are less dangerous than outside of the camps. Here, a boy plays with bottles outside his shelter.

The camp has a school. I go there three days a week with Achol and Joshua. Before, I did not go to school in my village. It was closed because of the war.

If we stay here, Grace, Luol, and my cousins can get an education. Grace is stronger now, but she is very quiet. Sometimes she just sits and stares. Sometimes she cries and cannot be comforted. Only Luol makes her smile and laugh. He is our funny boy. He is our joy.

A woman fills a cup with dirty water at a PoC camp in Juba.

## South Sudan's Story in Numbers

Around

# 200,000

people live in PoC camps in South Sudan. 61 percent of them are children.

# Challenges IDPs Face

People living in IDP camps in South Sudan face an uncertain future. They have lost everything. They have few possessions beyond the shirts on their backs. They hope that peace will come, and their homes will be safe enough to rebuild their lives.

Uganda has welcomed many refugees from South Sudan. There, refugees can work and move freely. The Bidi Bidi Camp in Uganda is one of the largest refugee camps in the world. It has more than 270,000 refugees. That is about the size of the city of Buffalo, New York.

A refugee carries a shelter package he was given when he arrived at the Bidi Bidi Camp in Uganda.

## UN Rights of the Child

Children have the right to the protection of their government.

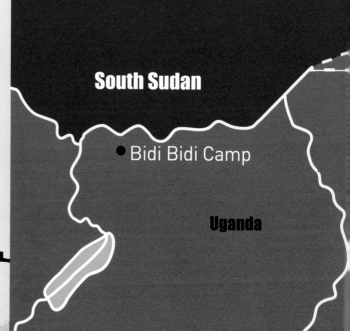

South Sudan

• Bidi Bidi Camp

Uganda

This man is using mud bricks to build a new home in Bidi Bidi Camp. His old home, in the background, was made from plastic sheeting and sticks.

Unlike a modern city, Bidi Bidi does not have paved roads, sewage systems, street lights, or other services. Refugees are given the material to build their own shelters. Aid agencies provide food and medical services. Refugees are good at making something out of very little. Some refugees have opened businesses at the camp. They sell food, clothing, and cell phones. Some make clothing or furniture to sell.

Few refugees make their way to Europe or North America. Those that do must adjust to different cultures, languages, and climates, or the regular weather in an area. Many suffer from the **trauma** of war. In South Sudan, the government does not help protect the people. Because of this, it can be difficult for refugees to trust police and authority figures when they live in other places.

# You Can Help!

South Sudan's people have suffered a lot. There are things you can do to help them, whether they are refugees or IDPs.

 With an adult's help, do some Internet research on aid organizations that help the people of South Sudan. Oxfam, Care, the United Nations International Children's Fund (UNICEF), and many others help people inside and outside of the country.

 Ask your family and friends to help you raise funds for these or other organizations. You could hold a bake sale or a used toy and book sale. Give the money you raise to the organization of your choice.

 Be friendly with a refugee going to your school or living in your neighborhood. Learn about their culture and help them learn about yours.

 Write to your local state or federal government representative. Tell them you are concerned about the safety of children who live in South Sudan. Ask them to speak out about the violence.

## UN Rights of the Child

Children from minority groups have the right to practice their religion and culture without fear of persecution.

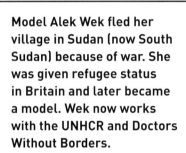

Model Alek Wek fled her village in Sudan (now South Sudan) because of war. She was given refugee status in Britain and later became a model. Wek now works with the UNHCR and Doctors Without Borders.

## Discussion Prompts

1. What are the differences between an internally displaced person, a refugee, and an immigrant?
2. Why is it important to help the people of South Sudan live together in their country?
3. Should governments work with aid organizations to help refugees?

29

# Glossary

**abuse** Cruel or violent treatment

**aid organizations** Organizations that help people who are in need due to war, poverty, or natural disasters

**assaulted** Physically attacked and harmed

**cholera** A disease that is spread by infected water supplies

**civil wars** Wars between groups of people in the same country

**conflicts** Struggles or battles

**empires** Groups of countries under a single ruler

**ethnic groups** Groups of people who have the same nation, culture, and religion

**exploitation** A practice of taking advantage of a person or using them unfairly

**famine** When there is not enough food in a certain area, which causes illness and death

**homeland** The country where someone was born or grew up

**immigrants** People who leave one country to live in another

**independent** Free of outside control

**internally displaced persons (IDPs)** People who are forced from their homes during a conflict, but remain in their country

**invaded** Taken over by armed forces

**militia** A military force made up of non-military members

**millet** A type of cereal grain

**peacekeepers** Military members who keep the peace between warring groups to keep people safe

**rations** A set amount of food and goods given to people regularly to keep them alive

**rebel** A person who fights against the government of a country

**refugees** People who flee from their own country to another due to unsafe conditions

**sewers** A ditch or pipe for carrying away human waste

**trauma** Emotional wounds or scary experiences that people have suffered, and that sometimes lead to long-term suffering

**United Nations (UN)** An international organization that promotes peace between countries and helps refugees

# Learning More

## Books
Morneau, Clare. *Kakuma Girls: Sharing Stories of Hardship and Hope from Kakuma Refugee Camp*. Barlow Book Publishing, 2016.

Owings, Lisa. *South Sudan* (Exploring Countries). Bellwether Media, 2012.

Solway, Andrew. *Graphing War and Conflict*. Capstone Publishing, 2010.

Williams, Mary. *Brothers in Hope: The Story of the Lost Boys of Sudan*. Lee & Low Books, 2005.

## Websites
**www.ducksters.com/kidsnews/south_sudan_new_country.php**
Find out more about the formation of South Sudan.

**http://easyscienceforkids.com/all-about-sudan-and-south-sudan**
This website provides bite-sized information on Sudan and South Sudan.

**www.unicef.org/rightsite/files/uncrcchilldfriendlylanguage.pdf**
Learn more about the United Nations Convention on the Rights of the Child.

**www.unrefugees.org/what-is-a-refugee**
Learn more about what it means to be a refugee and an IDP.

# Index

## About the Author

Ellen Rodger is a descendant of refugees who fled persecution
and famine. She has written and edited many books for children
and adults on subjects as varied as potatoes, how government
works, social justice, war, soccer, and lice and fleas.